Hello!

If this book is lost and you find it, please contact

_____
at
_____
to return it.

Thanks!

I Am Diversity
Exploring Race

by Tina Anderson

Tina Anderson
www.iam-diversity.com
info@iam-diversity.com

Copyright © 2019 by Tina Anderson
First printing 2020

ISBN-13: 978-1-7352260-0-2

All rights reserved. No part of this book may be used or reproduced in any manner whatsoever without the written permission of the author, except for brief quotations embodied in critical articles, educational assignments, reviews and writings on related subjects. For information regarding permission, go to *www.iam-diversity.com*.

The publisher and author do not have any control over and do not assume any responsibility for third-party websites or their content.

Edited by Manda Newlin
Cover design and layout by Dayna Offutt

*For my only child
Caleb*

*You are my greatest gift
from God*

May we and future generations live in a world filled with love and peace

v // I AM DIVERSITY: EXPLORING RACE

Contents

I Am African American 2
I Am Asian American 8
I Am Caucasian 14
I Am Hispanic 20
I Am Native American 26
I Am 32
Questions 34
The Student Pledge for All Children 35
Vocabulary. 36
Advocate and Become a Sponsor 40
Meet the Author 41
Images Cited 42
Notes 46

1 // I AM DIVERSITY: EXPLORING RACE

2 // I AM DIVERSITY: EXPLORING RACE

I Am
African American

The historical figures pictured on this page match the order in which they appear in this chapter.

3 // I AM DIVERSITY: EXPLORING RACE

I'm the only me I know
I'm the only me I see
All around
People frown
Without ever getting to know me

They watch the news
And then make rules
That everyone's the same
They think the worst
For truth they don't thirst
And they don't feel any shame

They see my facial features
And think my shoulder has a chip[1]
They think less of me
Because my ancestors arrived on a certain type of ship

I talked to my family
Because I wanted to cry
Why do people judge me
Oh why oh why

My family told me things
That I needed to hear
Many things made me smile
And many things made me cheer

---

1. Phrase from the nineteenth century in the U.S. based on people carrying a chip of wood on their shoulder and daring anyone to knock it off

Like Martin Luther King, Jr.
Had a dream
That people wouldn't be judged
By the color of their skin
But rather would be judged
By their character within

Harriet Tubman, aka Black Moses,
Traveled to Canada with a focus
Several times from the U.S. she made trips
To free hundreds who
Felt the cruelty of a country that used slave ships

Drivers in cars not knowing when to go
There was a need to help the cars flow
Traffic accidents all in sight
Garrett Morgan invented the three-position traffic light

Madam C.J. Walker accomplished much
Showing hair's versatility with a different touch
Wherever she went
People stopped and stared
Because she was the first woman millionaire

Alexander Miles perfected the elevator
So people could get to their destination
Sooner than later

Sojourner Truth, born a slave
Determined to be free
Sought equal rights
For Blacks and women in society
A preacher and an abolitionist, too
She changed her name from Isabella Van Wagener
And traveled for what was true

History is full of life lessons
And compels me to have
Better expressions
Of self-love, self-pride
And self-worth
No matter how many people throw me dirt

I have learned
That life isn't fair
And there is nothing
To dread about my hair

People who have skin like me
Hair like me
And facial features like me
Contribute to society
Just like me

I now use my haters as elevators
To get to the next level
I have a good head on my shoulders
And I'm not a rebel

6 // I AM DIVERSITY: EXPLORING RACE

I will say it loud:
I'm Black
And I'm proud.[2]

---

2. I'm Black and I'm Proud: words from the James Brown song, "Say It Loud – I'm Black and I'm Proud (Parts 1 & 2)." *A Soulful Christmas*. King Records, 1968.

7 // I AM DIVERSITY: EXPLORING RACE

8 // I AM DIVERSITY: EXPLORING RACE

I Am
Asian American

The historical figures pictured on this page match the order in which they appear in this chapter.

With my full eyes
I see the whole picture
Never mind people
Who place Asians on one fixture

There's a lot to being Asian
We're not all Chinese
And yes we are polite
We like to say please

I talked to my family
Because I wanted to understand
Why stereotyping people
Is a part of others' plan

My family and friends say it's not right
To place everyone in the same boat
Ignoring ignorance
Is how we must float

To rise above occasions
In this great nation
We took a walk through history
To unfog the mystery

Michiko Kakutani
Reported the news with integrity
Through great leaps and bounds
A literary critic who kept her nose around

With a hard punch and kick
That were so good
Bruce Lee took it
To Hollywood
He showed the world
That it was just fine
To have a leading Asian
Saying the lines
Lee gave hope to young boys
With their action-packed toys
Not limited to a grocer or other pigeonhole
Children saw new hope from new opportunities unfold

Inventor An Wang was on a mission
He used engineering to create a new system
He helped design the first fully electronic computer
Welcome to the world of technology
And a brighter future

11 // I AM DIVERSITY: EXPLORING RACE

Patsy Mink, first nonwhite woman to serve in Congress
Unequal athletic opportunities she helped put to rest
After all, female athletes deserved a shot
Title IX silenced opposers who tried to say what girls are not

Young-Oak Kim applied to the U.S. Army in 1940
Only to sadly be told "No, sorry"
But a year later a change in law began
Allowing a group to serve the country – Asian Americans

Colonel Kim read maps for impossible missions to meet
He was up to the challenge
He didn't accept defeat
Kim said, "We're all Americans and we're fighting for the same cause"
His eternal words of unity deserve the biggest applause
Kim was the first minority officer who at his hand
Was an army combat battalion following his command

Maxine Hong Kingston put stereotypes to rest
In fact she showed *China Men*[3] at their best
While others painted Chinese men in a bad way
With a stroke of a new brush
She said what she had to say

---

3. *China Men* is Maxine Hong Kingston's collection of stories about three generations of Chinese men in America

I see that one person can impact the world
I want to inspire every boy and girl
To look at the things of the past
And set a new trail of love that lasts

As the largest population in the world
We know how to live
Words of wisdom
We freely give.

13 // I AM DIVERSITY: EXPLORING RACE

14 // I AM DIVERSITY: EXPLORING RACE

I Am Caucasian

The historical figures pictured on this page match the order in which they appear in this chapter.

Many in this country look like me
The largest group
In the U.S.
Yet different ancestry

People say we don't try at all
To understand nonwhites
We enjoy White privilege
And we're not polite

I talked to my family
Because I wanted to understand
Why do people keep telling me
That I'm the man

My family said that I, too, am a victim
Yet in the reverse
Discrimination is an evil
Something to curse

They reminded me that I feed myself
Never a silver spoon
I reach for the stars
And fly to the moon

My family further explained
A vast history lesson
Rights done in this country
And cause for celebration

George Washington was a founding father with a vision
He knew the power of unity when making a decision
Coming together as one made a lot of sense
Under the newly formed constitution, he was the first
United States President

Steve Jobs was his own boss
An entrepreneur
A genius in the world of the computer
He and his partners built a dream from a garage
The creation of Apple without a facade

The first solo female aviator across the Atlantic Ocean
Amelia Earhart put her dream into motion
She started an organization to help other female pilots
Become greater
A key message: don't postpone your dreams until later

Walt Disney was a pioneer in animation
Cartoons became every kid's fascination
Visual learning that was fun all the time
He helped amusement park in our minds

17 // I AM DIVERSITY: EXPLORING RACE

Hillary Clinton
A woman on a mission
As First Lady and U.S. Senator
She did a lot of things great
And powerful words she spoke in several debates
She showed that you can prevail if within yourself you are free
In 2016 she was the first female presidential candidate
Nominated by a major party

Helen Keller was the first deaf-blind person to earn a BA degree
Her approach said I create my path to success even if
I can't hear or see
Work harder if you must
But make no excuses at all
Go under and over blockage
Get around the wall

I learned a lot
From lessons about history
In spite of what others think
I can be the best me

Some of my ancestors did right
While others did wrong
I write lyrics for my own life
In a new song

I choose to learn about others
And show them who I am
My hope is we can all live united
In this blessed land.

19 // I AM DIVERSITY: EXPLORING RACE

20 // I AM DIVERSITY: EXPLORING RACE

I Am Hispanic

The historical figures pictured on this page match the order in which they appear in this chapter.

When I look in the mirror
I know what I see
Yet people around
Constantly judge me

My feelings have been so hurt
That I don't know what to do
Why are people so mean
Without ever getting to know you

Thankfully I have
Family and friends
Who are there for me
Through thick and thin

At times when I'm hurt
And don't know
What to say
They are there
To lead the way

Mi familia y amigos
Speak above the crowd
The words they say
Speak to my heart loud
I come from a race
With great pride
That works hard
And takes things in stride

Sonia Sotomayor
Did much to adore
Latina Supreme Court Justice
She was the first
Doing right is what
She wanted people to thirst

César Chávez knew
What it meant to farm
He disliked conditions
Causing workers harm
Through nonviolent means
To make wages right
Improving working conditions
Is how he dedicated his life

Linda Chavez-Thompson,
Once vice president at AFSCME
And also vice chairperson of
The Democratic National Committee
A translator who worked hard and not for show
She was also the first person of color
To serve as executive vice president
Of the AFL-CIO

Ernesto Galarza
First low-income Mexican American
To graduate from college
Accomplished much
For others to pay homage
The first union
Of multiracial farmers
He did organize
And in 1976 in literature
He was nominated for the Nobel Prize

In government
Antonia Coello Novello
Had empowerment
She was a lady
On a mission
First woman to hold
The U.S. Surgeon General position

General Elwood "Pete" Quesada
Helped create
A means for airline safety
To no longer await
He helped start
The Federal Aviation Agency
He was a man with a purpose
And worked faithfully

In the U.S., I see me and you
This is my country, too
I will say it once again
Es mi país también.

25 // I AM DIVERSITY: EXPLORING RACE

26 // I AM DIVERSITY: EXPLORING RACE

I Am
Native American

The historical figures pictured on this page match the order in which they appear in this chapter.

27 // I AM DIVERSITY: EXPLORING RACE

I was here in the beginning
Yet people wrote my ending
Their egos try to swell
But I say, "Oh well"

I don't understand
This is not right
How can people judge me
Even at first sight

I rely on the wisdom of elders
Family and friends
To help me overcome
The harsh looks I see again and again

A journey through history
Accomplishments from the past
Show that what really happens
Are the things that last

Not someone's false assumption
Or stereotype
I choose to believe the truth
And not the hype

I behold
The signal
And with the truth
I mingle

25 years fighting for the land
Every force from every hand
"Take my land? Oh, no!"
These were the actions of Geronimo

Mourning Dove
Had a heart filled with love
To make right ways stick
She engaged in tribal politics

Toypurina fought
To stop violence and forced labor
Her actions indicated the time is now
Don't you dare wait for a savior

Sitting Bull
Took every ounce of strength he could muster
And at the Battle of Little Bighorn
He defeated General Custer

Sequoyah saw a need
To help people communicate
Therefore a writing system
He did create
A new way
For people to write freely
He created
The Cherokee Syllabary

Nanyehi (pronounced Nan-yi)
Beloved Cherokee woman
Who didn't watch time go by
She wasn't afraid to fight
After her husband was killed in battle
She fought to stop the plight
She also negotiated
For the Treaty of Holston
Reminding U.S. treaty commissioners
"We are your mothers;
You are our sons"

From the shore of my heart
I have a fresh start
I'm on a war-trail
And I will not fail

From challenges each year
I will not fear
I can't major in minors
My life. My future. I'm the designer.

31 // I AM DIVERSITY: EXPLORING RACE

I Am

I stopped letting mean people
Get me down
I willingly go forward
Knowing that I am bound
To succeed
And to be
The best that I can possibly be

Each race is different
From the rest
Can society embrace diversity
Is the test

I will.

Questions

1. What did you learn by reading this book? What can you use in your life?

2. A stereotype is the act of making conclusions about others based on personal beliefs about them. What evidence in this book of poetry can you find on stereotypes?

3. How do personal beliefs affect how people react to others from different backgrounds?

4. This book focuses on racial diversity. What are some other ways that make people different?

5. Why should you know facts about the person who first achieved something? How can knowing the facts help you?

6. How can people be more open to getting to know others from different backgrounds?

7. What are some mean things that people do or say to others who are different? What can you do to stop wrongs from happening?

Join the Movement for Social Change

Download a printable certificate at www.iam-diversity.com

The Student Pledge for All Children

When interacting with others, I pledge to respect them and have an open mind. Although others are different than me, I pledge to treat them with the same high regard that I treat myself.

Vocabulary

Diversity: the state of being different

African American
- **ancestors:** family members of long ago who came before you
- **versatility:** flexibility; ability to easily change
- **sojourner:** a person who lives in one place for a short time
- **abolitionist:** a person who is against an evil such as slavery
- **dread:** fear or not look forward to

Asian American
- **fixture:** something that stays in place
- **stereotyping:** making conclusions about others based on personal beliefs about them
- **ignorance:** not knowing certain information
- **critic:** a person who shares his or her expertise or opinion about something
- **pigeonhole:** a label, group or class, usually negative
- **engineering:** a career in which people use natural resources to help others; constructing a road is an example
- **opposers:** people who are against others or their ideas
- **battalion:** a large body of troops in a military branch such as the army

Caucasian American
- **ancestry:** family members of long ago who came before you
- **privilege:** idea that someone gets something without earning it
- **discrimination:** treating people worse than others without a fair reason
- **vast:** big

- **constitution:** the laws for a country and the basic rights for its citizens
- **entrepreneur:** a person who works for himself or herself
- **facade:** a false or misleading appearance
- **aviator:** a person who flies aircraft
- **pioneer:** a person who is among the first to explore something
- **nominate:** recommend someone for a special award or position
- **major party:** a political group that can get enough votes to win control of the government; in the U.S., the two major parties are the Democratic Party and the Republican Party
- **BA degree:** short for bachelor of arts degree or a four-year degree at a college or university in which the student earns credits in liberal arts subjects

Hispanic
- **Latina:** a female who was born in or lives in Latin America or has Latin ancestry
- **Supreme Court Justice:** a member of the highest court in the U.S.
- **AFSCME:** American Federation of State, County and Municipal Employees; currently the largest and fastest-growing public services union, with members from hundreds of different occupations
- **Democratic National Committee:** a group that governs the Democratic Party; it was formed during the 1848 Democratic National Convention and is the oldest continuing party committee in the U.S.

- **AFL-CIO:** American Federation of Labor and Congress of Industrial Organizations; "the largest federation of unions in the United States. It is made up of 55 national and international unions, together representing more than 12 million active and retired workers."[4]
- **homage:** respect
- **union:** as in labor union; a group of workers that seeks to protect the rights of its members and meet their interests on pay, working conditions and benefits
- **Nobel Prize:** an award given out each year to encourage people who work for the interest of others
- **empowerment:** the act of giving power to someone
- **U.S. Surgeon General:** a governmental position; this person heads the U.S. Public Health Service Commissioned Corps and is the leading spokesperson about public health in the U.S.
- **Federal Aviation Agency:** an organization in the U.S. Department of Transportation that is responsible for the safety of operating and flying civilian aircraft

Spanish Words
- **mi familia y amigos:** my family and friends
- **es mi país también:** it's my country, too

Native American
- **egos:** the opinions people have about who they are or their abilities
- **muster:** gather or bring together

---

4. "AFL-CIO." Wikipedia. https://en.wikipedia.org/wiki/AFL-CIO. Accessed Aug. 25, 2020.

- **syllabary:** a form of writing in which a symbol represents a syllable and not just a consonant or vowel; Cherokee is an example
- **plight:** a difficult situation
- **U.S. treaty commissioners:** people who guide groups to reach an agreement in which they all benefit and can exist together in harmony

BUY THE BOOK
Order copies of *I Am Diversity: Exploring Race*
by Tina Anderson

Amazon.com

ADVOCATE
Inform educators and organizations of the learning opportunities using *I Am Diversity: For Schools and Organizations*, including inviting Tina Anderson as a guest speaker

www.iam-diversity.com
info@iam-diversity.com

BECOME A SPONSOR
Express your interest in sponsoring an *I Am Diversity* event

www.iam-diversity.com
info@iam-diversity.com

MEET THE AUTHOR

TINA ANDERSON was born and raised in Fort Wayne, Ind. She developed an early love for reading and writing. During elementary and middle school, teachers selected her as a young author.

After earning a bachelor's degree in business management from Indiana State University, Tina moved to Indianapolis, Ind. She later earned a four-year degree in English education from Indiana University Purdue University Indianapolis (IUPUI).

Tina is a freelance writer and editor. *I Am Diversity: Exploring Race* is Tina's first published book. More books in the series are forthcoming.

Images Cited

43 // I AM DIVERSITY: EXPLORING RACE

Images Cited

African American

1. *Martin Luther King, Jr. Pixabay.* Photo. Accessed Aug. 22, 2020.

2. Powelson, Benjamin F. *Carte-de-visite showing a considerably younger Harriet Tubman than normally seen in the known images of her, just coming off her work during the Civil War.* Between 1868 and 1869. *Wikimedia Commons.* Photo. Accessed Aug. 23, 2020.

3. Photographer unknown. *Garrett Morgan.* Date unknown. *Wikipedia.* Photo. Accessed Aug. 27, 2020.

4. Scurlock Studio. *Madam C.J. Walker.* Circa 1914. *Wikimedia Commons.* Photo. Accessed Aug. 22, 2020.

5. Photographer unknown. *Alexander Miles of Duluth Minnesota.* Circa 1895. *Wikimedia Commons.* Photo. Accessed Aug. 23, 2020.

6. Randall Studio. Sojourner Truth. Circa 1870. *Wikimedia Commons.* Photo. Accessed Aug. 23, 2020.

Asian American

1. Tribeca Disruptive Innovation. *Michiko Kakutani at Tribeca Disruptive Innovation.* 2018. *Wikimedia Commons.* Photo. Accessed Aug. 22, 2020.

2. National General Pictures. *Photo of Bruce Lee from the film Fists of Fury (aka The Big Boss).* 1973. *Wikimedia Commons.* Photo. Accessed Aug. 22, 2020.

3. A graphic illustration of An Wang was created for this project.

4. Patterson, Laura. *U.S. Representative Patsy Mink Announcing Creation of C.A.P.A.C.* 1994. Library of Congress Prints and Photographs Division Washington, D.C. *Flickr.* Photo. Accessed Aug. 22, 2020.

5. Go for Broke National Education Center. *Portrait image of Lieutenant Colonel Young-Oak Kim wearing his Dress Blue uniform.* 1961. *Wikipedia.* Photo. Accessed Aug. 22, 2020.

6. Shankbone, David. *Maxine Hong Kingston in New York City.* 2006. *Wikimedia Commons.* Photo. Accessed Aug. 22, 2020.

Caucasian

1. Pendleton's Lithography. *George Washington*. Circa 1828. Library of Congress Prints & Photographs Division. Washington, D.C. *Unsplash*. Lithograph printed by Pendleton's Lithography from an original series painted by Gilbert Stuart. Accessed Aug. 22, 2020.

2. Photographer unknown. *Steve Jobs 1955-2011*. 2011. *Flickr*. Photo. Accessed Aug. 27, 2020.

3. Harris & Ewing. *Amelia Earhart in airplane*. 1936. Library of Congress Prints and Photographs Division. Washington, D.C. *Wikipedia*. Photo. Accessed Aug. 22, 2020.

4. Boy Scouts of America. *Publicity Photo of Walt Disney*. 1946. *Wikimedia*. Photo. Accessed Aug. 22, 2020.

5. U.S. Department of State. *Official Portrait of Secretary of State Hillary Clinton*. 2009. *Wikimedia*. Photo. Accessed Aug. 22, 2020.

6. Family member of Thaxter P. Spencer. *Photograph of Helen Keller at age 8 with her tutor Anne Sullivan on vacation in Brewster, Cape Cod, Massachusetts*. 1888. R. Stanton Avery Special Collections, at the New England Historic Genealogical Society. *Wikimedia*. Photo. Accessed Aug. 22, 2020.

Hispanic

1. Photographer unknown. *Sonia Sotomayor, U.S. Supreme Court Justice*. 2009. Collection of the Supreme Court of the United States. *Wikipedia*. Photo. Accessed Aug. 22, 2020.

2. Levine, Joel. *César Chávez – speaking at the Delano UFW–United Farm Workers rally in Delano, California*. 1972. *Wikimedia Commons*. Photo. Accessed Aug. 22, 2020.

3. SpaceRocker Photograph by Michael Steenbergen. *Linda Chavez-Thompson at the Cimarron Club in Mission Texas at a meeting with the Hidalgo County Texas Democratic Women as she campaigns for Texas Lieutenant Governor*. 2010. *Wikimedia Commons*. Photo. Accessed Aug. 22, 2020.

4. Photographer unknown. *Ernesto Galarza*. Date unknown. *Wikipedia*. Photo. Accessed Aug. 27, 2020.

5. U.S. Department of Health and Human Services. *Vice Admiral Antonia C. Novello, M.D., M.P.H., Dr.P.H. (USPHS); 14th Surgeon General of the United States.* Date unknown. *Wikimedia Commons.* Photo. Accessed Aug. 22, 2020.

6. A U.S. Army employee. *Pete Quesada.* Date unknown. *Wikipedia.* Photo. Accessed Aug. 22, 2020.

Native American

1. Photographer unknown. *Portrait of Apache chief Geronimo with his bow and arrow.* Before 1909. AGN collection. *Wikipedia.* Photo. Accessed Aug. 22, 2020.

2. Photographer unknown. *Portrait of Native American author Mourning Dove.* 1915. American Indians of the Pacific Northwest Collection at the Northwest Museum of Arts and Culture. *Wikipedia.* Photo. Accessed Aug. 22, 2020.

3. A graphic illustration of Toypurina was created for this project.

4. Barry, David F. *Sitting Bull.* Circa 1883. Daniel Guggisberg historical photographs collection. *Wikimedia Commons.* Photo. Accessed Aug. 22, 2020.

5. Lehman, George and Peter S. Duval, lithographers. Inman, Henry, painter. Copy after a painting by Charles Bird King. *Sequoyah with a tablet depicting his writing system for the Cherokee language.* 19th century. *Wikimedia.* Lithograph. Accessed Aug. 27, 2020.

6. A graphic illustration of Nanyehi was created for this project.

NOTES

NOTES

NOTES

NOTES

www.ingramcontent.com/pod-product-compliance
Lightning Source LLC
LaVergne TN
LVHW051512070426
835507LV00022B/3078